I0816178

THE AMAZING FOODS OF AFRICA: A TO Z

DR. ARTIKA R. TYNER
DORTHY GBOLO

Illustrations by Reyhana Ismail
Design by Reyhana Ismail

All inquiries or sales requests should be addressed to:

Planting People Growing Justice Press
P.O. Box 131894
Saint Paul, MN 55113
www.ppgjli.org

Printed and bound in the United States of America

First Edition
LCCN: 2024932611
1-9781959223535-11/1/2024

This book is dedicated to our foremothers who showed love through their cooking.

MAP OF AFRICA

A is for Attiéké.

Attiéké is made from cassava roots and is eaten with stews and soups in many parts of West Africa.

is for Beans.

There are more than fifty types of bean dishes that are made and eaten all over the continent of Africa.

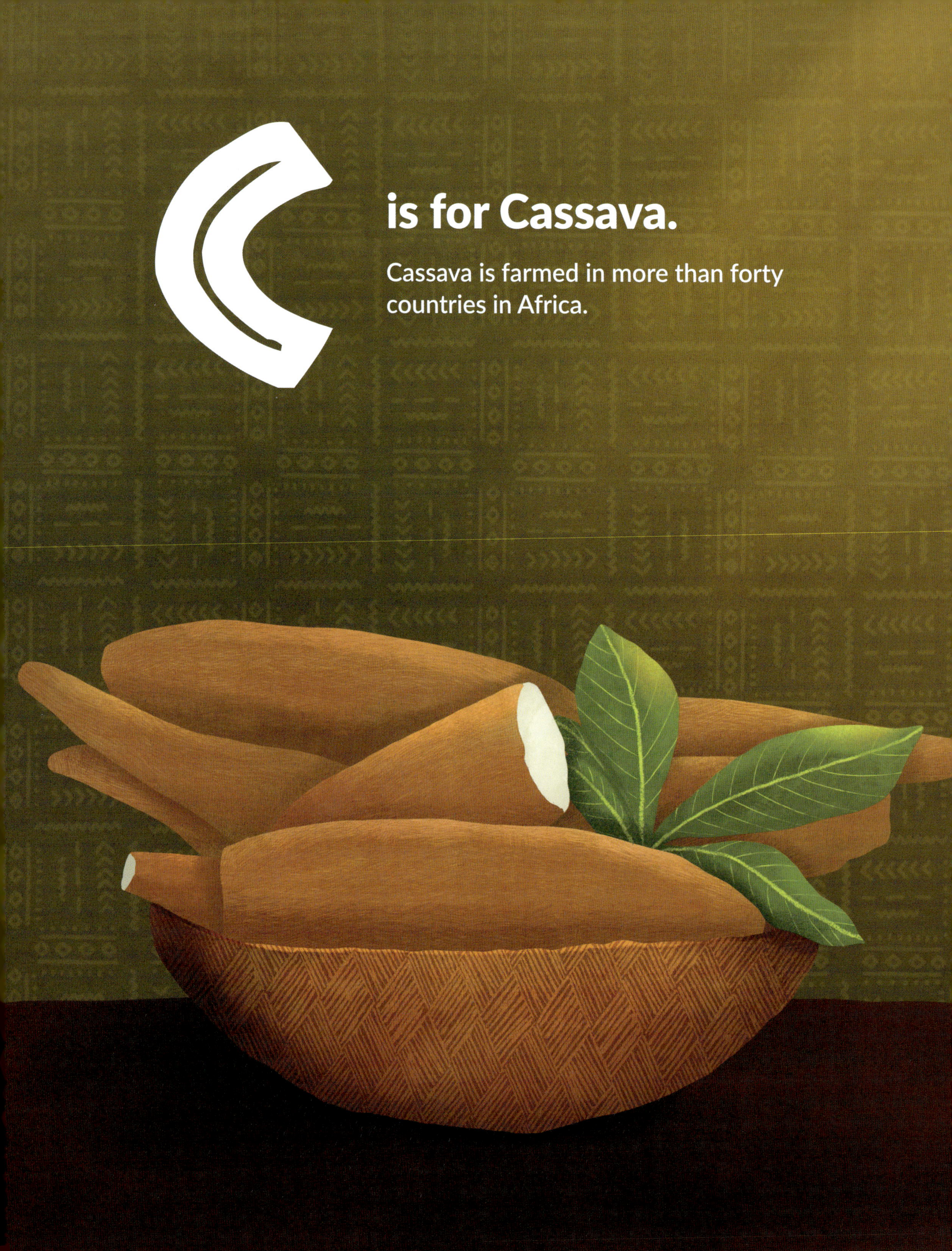

C is for Cassava.

Cassava is farmed in more than forty countries in Africa.

is for Dambou.

Dambou is a dish that comes from Niger made from rice flour, couscous, or grains.

is for Egusi Soup.

Egusi soup is made with the seeds of melons, squash, or gourds, palm oil, beef stock, pumpkin leaves, and water leaves. This dish is very popular in Nigeria.

is for Family.

Family is the foundation of community and unity all across Africa.

"A united family eats from the same plate."

G is for Goat.

Goats are a farmer's best friend.

African farmers use their hides for leather, milk for cheese and butter, and the meat to make delicious goat stew.

is for Hausa Koko.

Hausa koko is a spicy porridge made from grain and seasoned with salt, ginger, cloves, and hot chili powder. It is usually eaten for breakfast.

I is for Injera.

Injera is an Ethiopian flatbread made with teff, barley or wheat flour, yeast, and water. Enjoy it with your favorite African stew.

is for Jollof Rice.

Jollof rice is a popular dish across West Africa. There are even competitions for the best Jollof around the world. Which country should be the winner?

is for Kala.

Kala is a Liberian fried treat that can be eaten plain, dipped in sugar, or with pepper sauce. This dish has many names across West Africa, such as puff puff and bofrot.

is for Lamb.

Lamb is farmed throughout Africa. The wool is used for clothes and the meat is roasted and made into stews.

M is for Matoke Bananas.

Matoke bananas are a bright green fruit. Once peeled, they can be boiled, steamed, or mashed and are used in many dishes in Central Africa.

N is for Ndolé.

Ndolé is a peanut stew made with ground peanuts, onions, spices, stock, and lots of bitter leaf that gives it its signature green color. This dish can be found in Cameroon.

is for Okra.

Okra is a key part of many dishes in West Africa and can be cooked in many different ways.

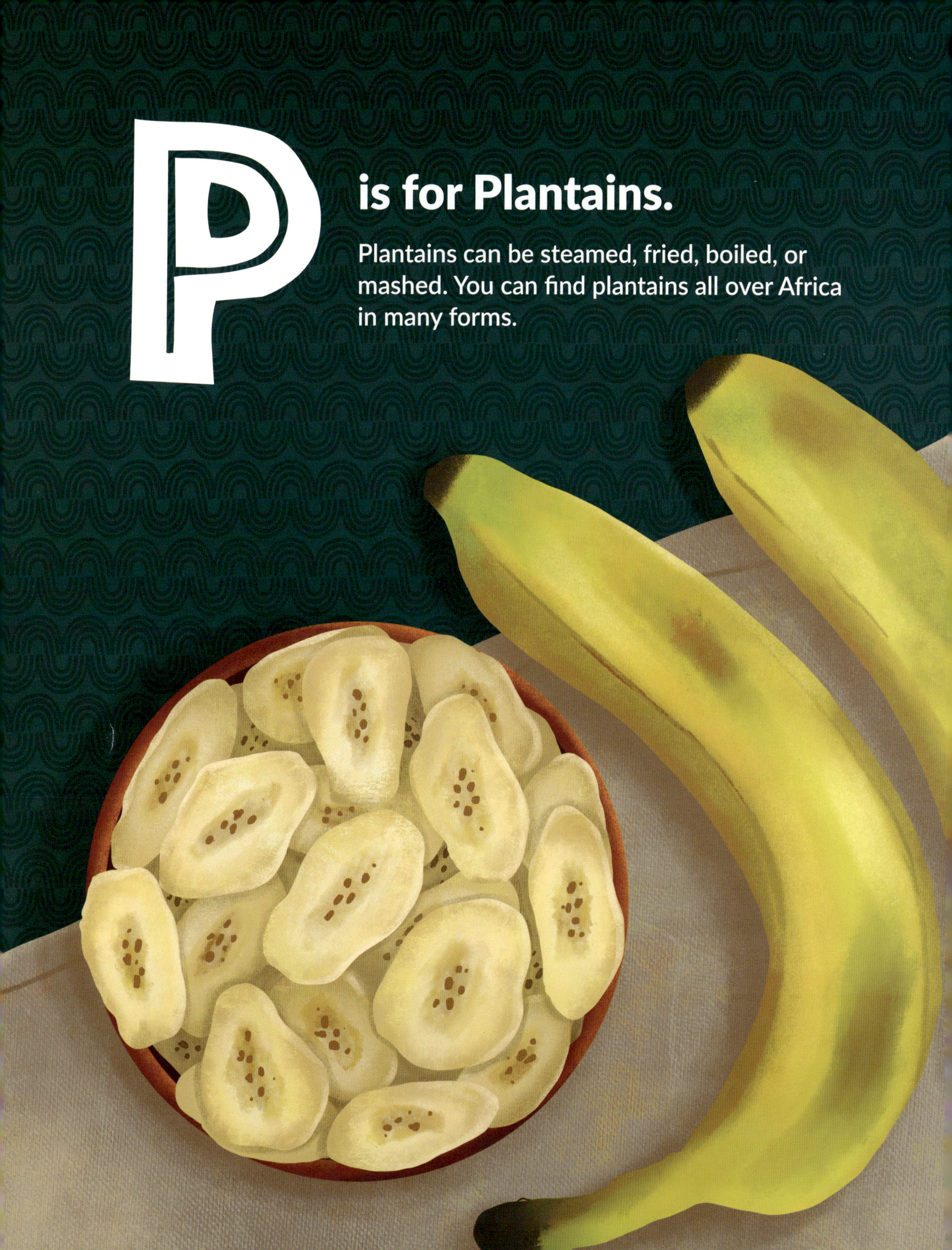

P is for Plantains.

Plantains can be steamed, fried, boiled, or mashed. You can find plantains all over Africa in many forms.

Q is for Qatayef.

Qatayef is a sweet dessert mostly eaten during Ramadan. This very thin pancake is filled with a sweet cream, rolled in pistachios, and drizzled with a sweet syrup.

is for Rice.

Rice is the foundation of many meals across Africa.

is for Stew.

Stew is the main style of cooking all across Africa. Stews are made of meats, vegetables, and fresh spices.

T is for Tangia.

Tangia is a unique dish made by cooking lamb in a clay urn with fresh spices. This is a Moroccan specialty.

is for Umngqusho.

Umngqusho is a common South African side dish made with beans and dried corn.

V is for Vetkoek.

Vetkoek is a street food. It is also called "fat cake" and is made with cake flour, sugar, and salt. You can eat it sweet with jam and cheese or savory with your favorite meat.

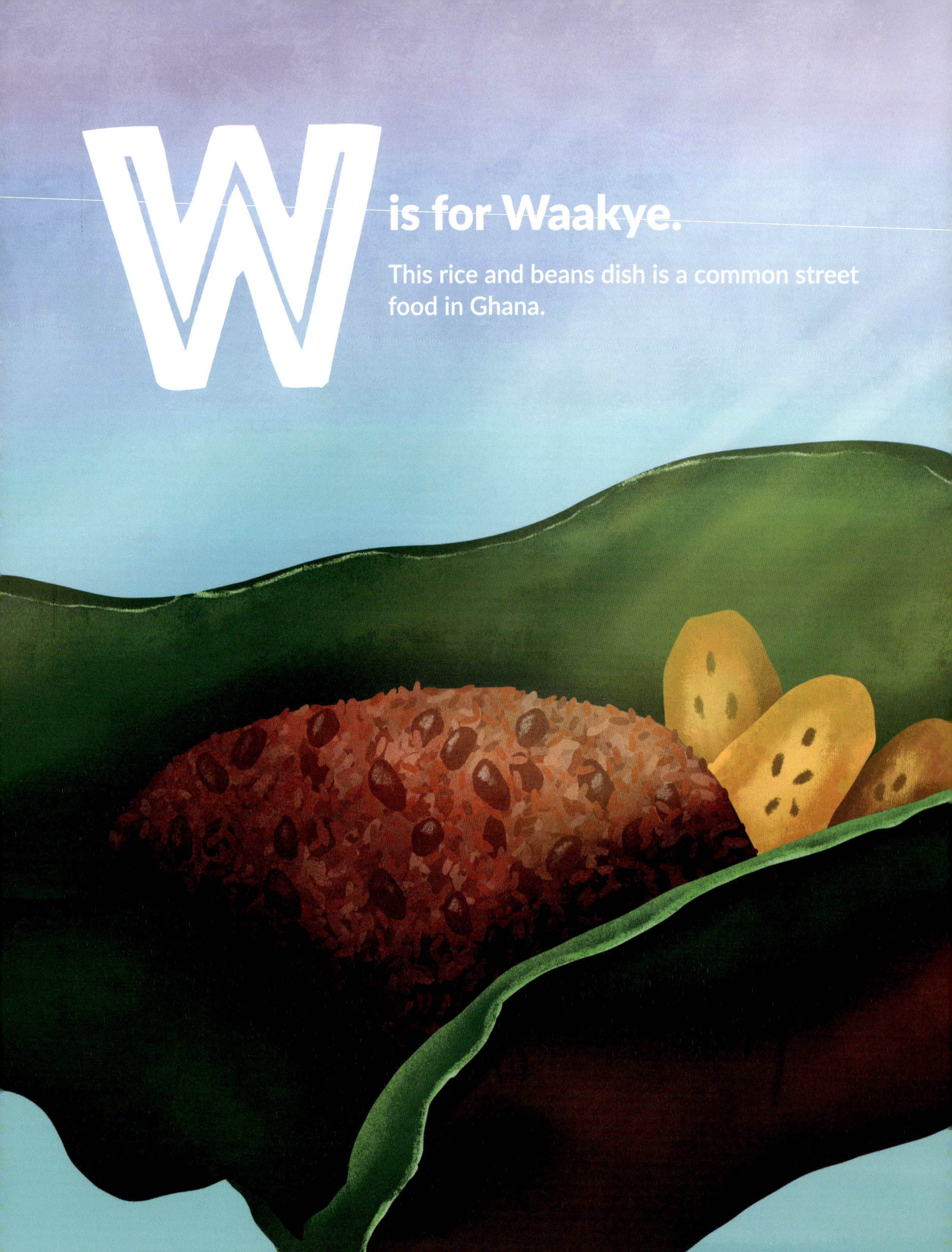

W is for Waakye.

This rice and beans dish is a common street food in Ghana.

X is for for Ximenia Caffra.

Ximenia caffra is a fruit tree that can be found all over East Africa. The tree produces a sour plum-like fruit that is used in jams and desserts.

Y is for Yassa.

Yassa is Senegal's national dish. It is an onion stew that can be paired with your favorite meat and enjoyed with rice.

Z is for Zobo.

Zobo is a tea made of Zobo leaves, pineapple juice, ginger, turmeric, cloves, and cinnamon.

LIST OF COUNTRIES (A-Z)

A is for Algeria and Angola

B is for Benin, Botswana, Burkina Faso, and Burundi

C is for Cameroon, Cape Verde, Central African Republic, Chad, Comoros, Democratic Republic of the Congo, Republic of the Congo and Cote d'Ivoire

D is for Djibouti

E is for Egypt, Equatorial Guinea, Eritrea, and Ethiopia

G is Gabon, Gambia, Ghana, Guinea, and Guinea Bissau

K is for Kenya

L is for Lesotho, Liberia, and Libya

M is for Madagascar, Malawi, Mali, Mauritania, Mauritius, Morocco, and Mozambique

N is for Namibia, Niger, and Nigeria

R is for Rwanda

S is for Sao Tome and Principe, Senegal, Seychelles, Sierra Leone, Somalia, South Africa, South Sudan, Sudan, and Swaziland

T is Tanzania, Togo, and Tunisia

U is for Uganda

Z is for Zambia and Zimbabwe

FAMOUS AFRICAN CHEFS

Marcus Samuelsson is an Ethiopian-born chef. You might recognize him from a few cooking shows on TV like *Chopped*, *Iron Chef*, and many more. He has written eight cookbooks. He has helped bring African cuisine to a worldwide scale.

Pierre Thiam is a Senegalese chef who specializes in West African cuisine. He is the executive chef of award-winning restaurants in Lagos, Nigeria, and Dakar, Senegal.

Siba Mtongana is a South African Food Network host and celebrity chef. She is also an entrepreneur who owns the Siba Company, which includes her restaurant. She is the author of the award-winning cookbook, *My Table*.

Nompumelelo Mqwebu is the author of *Through the Eyes of an African Chef*. She is a South African columnist who won the award for the world's best self-published cookbook in 2018. She is a food traveler who enjoys learning about food and using natural ingredients fresh from the farm.

AFRICAN PROVERBS

Good food goes with music. —African proverb

Eat when the food is ready. Speak when the time is right. —Ethiopian proverb

Ubuntu: A person is a person because of other people. —African proverb

DR. ARTIKA R. TYNER

Dr. Artika R. Tyner is a passionate educator, an award-winning author, a civil rights attorney, a sought-after speaker, and an advocate for justice who is committed to helping children discover their leadership potential and serve as change agents in the global community.

DORTHY GBOLO

Dorthy Gbolo is a first-generation Liberian American who calls St. Paul her home. Dorthy is an IT Support Specialist and an entrepreneur. Her catering business specializes in Liberian and African American cuisine, using both to bring the two communities together and provide an affordable alternative food option. In her free time, she enjoys reading and spending time with her family and friends.

ABOUT PLANTING PEOPLE GROWING JUSTICE LEADERSHIP INSTITUTE

Planting People Growing Justice Leadership Institute seeks to plant seeds of social change through education, training, and community outreach.

A portion of the proceeds from this book will support the educational programming of Planting People Growing Justice Leadership Institute. Learn more at www.ppgjli.org

Related Titles:

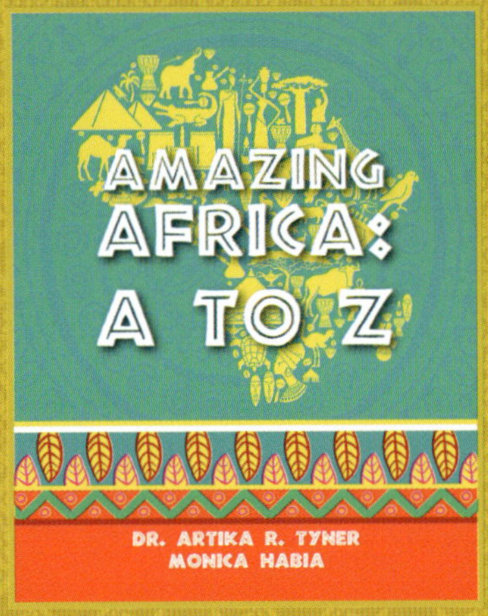

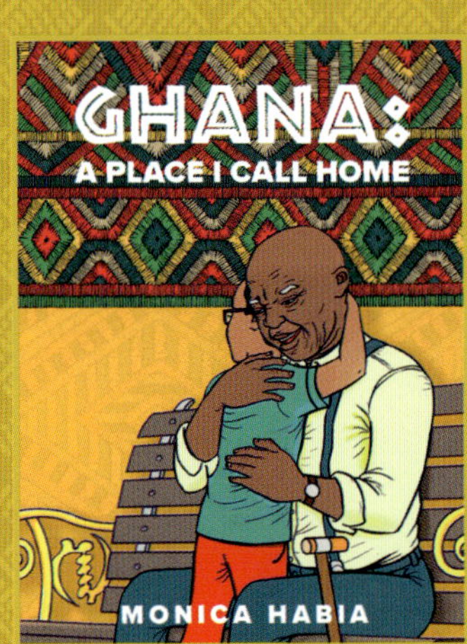